A BETTER WOMAN

10 tips that can help you become a better wife and save your marriage

Dr Kimberly Martin

TABLE OF CONTENTS

Catalog

INTRODUCTION

This book is for every woman out there trying so hard to save their relationships or marriages from crumbling. Inside the book you will find answers to your questions on becoming a better woman to your spouse.

Every woman deserves to be happy in their marriages or relationships, doing the right things at the right time will help in every way.

Don't be afraid to take the right step or make the right decision because it will help you build a successful relationship as this book will guild you in every attempt you make and will help you achieve your goal .

1. Carve out Some Opportunities to Rekindle the Lost Romance in Your Hectic Schedules

At the point when you become a mother, you have another person in your life and room whom you love. That doesn't mean you quit communicating your affection to your better half. Take part in things that satisfied you as a team before the child went along. Figure out some opportunity consistently, regardless of whether it is 5 minutes, to have a quiet talk about non-child things. Once more, begin dating.

2. Approach Him with Respect

Parenthood makes large numbers of us unnerving people. We are dependably confounded.

We are for the most part cantankerous, furious, miserable, befuddled, or disturbed - and frequently a blend of every one of these. Since the kid is still excessively little, it is not difficult to take everything out on your better half. It is not difficult to fault him for each little test you face. Try not to be that irritating, ridiculous spouse! Examine with him your difficulties. Be that as it may, do it smoothly, without censuring and pointing fingers.

Invest energy with him. Have a good time. Appreciate his conversation as a person. Focus on his words. Having ordinary date evenings is an unquestionable requirement, as I would like to think since they give you an opportunity to zero in on each other and your relationship. On the off chance that looking after children time away are an issue, evaluate one of the at-home date thoughts found in books you have perused or things you haves seen on the web

 Continuously attempt to be grateful. Try not to simply say "Thank You Dear." Thank him for explicit things - for making a garbage run, for cutting the grass, for making an exquisite supper. Say thanks to him frequently. That is one more approach to approaching him with deference. When enticed to condemn or utilize a cruel word or a harsh tone, simply attempt to hush up. Given the other option, quietness is the deferential decision.

3. Support His Work, Ambition and Vision

Dissimilar to previously, you probably won't have as much opportunity to discuss his goals and backing his vision. Despite the fact that you can't subscribe to his prosperity at this crossroads, you ought to keep on inspiring him to do things he cherishes. Make sure to get some information about his advancement. Attempt to assist him with carving out opportunity to follow his enthusiasm.

Research shows that consolation from better halves to seek after objectives in regions like profession, school, kinship, and wellness makes individuals bound to accomplish those objectives as a matter of fact.

Assuming they want to practice more, assist them with thinking of a particular arrangement and spotlight on objectives that are sensible and feasible. It's vital that these plans are explicit (e.g., run for 15 minutes on the treadmill before work), instead of general (e.g., practice 3 times each week).

Attempting to control your accomplice's activity can blow up. At the point when individuals feel like their opportunity to do what they is compromised, they will grip to that undermined opportunity more-like a kid who frantically needs to play with a particular toy just in light of the fact that it's prohibited. At the point when you attempt to control your accomplice, you are confining their opportunity.

Attempting to control your accomplice's activities can blow up. At the point when individuals feel like their opportunity to do what they need is being compromised, they'll grip to that undermined opportunity more — like a youngster who frantically needs to play with a particular toy essentially on the grounds that it's illegal. At the point when you attempt to control your accomplice, you're confining their opportunity.

Supporting your significant other's objectives could in some cases include pushing them BUT don't attempt to control them, and now and again it could expect you to pay attention to them. Some of the time you could likewise need to give them a motivational speech when they are feeling demotivated. Being a steady accomplice includes different cherishing and caring activities as they make progress toward their objectives.

4. Assist Him With nurturing

Dissimilar to moms, many dads are not normal at nurturing. On the off chance that you think he is taking a secondary lounge in nurturing, perhaps it is on the grounds that he probably won't understand what to do or how to help. It could likewise be on the grounds that you are attempting to do everything without anyone else giving him relatively few obligations as a parent. Anything that might be the situation, here is an opportunity to cooperate collectively. So, assist him with being a super-father by showing him basic undertakings like evolving nappies, taking care of and washing the kid and giving him obligations, he can do when he is near.

5. Ask His Priorities

Assuming you are baffled by how much work you do in the family, converse with him and ask him what his needs are. Does he really want lunch to be stuffed consistently? Could you at any point deal with doing his clothing just one time each week? Does he actually have to often associate with companions? Essentially, figure out his best 5 needs and attempt to consolidate them in your day-to-day routines. This won't just make his life simple; it will likewise show him you actually care bounty!

6. Focus on Him

Okay, we realize you can't do this consistently. In any case, every so often, plan his number one dinner and eat with him. Wear something, he enjoys. Offer him daily's reprieve. Do things that you realize will satisfy him. Furthermore, attempt to easily do this. Assuming you seem as though you are just with him face to face, however you are actually engrossed about child stuff, it wouldn't get the job done.

made butterflies in your stomach and you could grin when you even contemplated him? Recall when he was your reality? When you remained before him, alongside your companions, family, and God and promised to esteem him until the end of your life?

It was simple then, right? It was basic in those days to Make your better half fundamentally important. However, life has an approach to impeding you with obligations and plans for the day that are endless, and the most straightforward thing to set aside for later is your marriage, particularly assuming you have children. All things considered, your children couldn't address their own issues without your help, and your Spouse is a totally mature man who can deal with himself. It's normal that he gets shoved aside, sensible even.

What you search for you'll see. What's more, assuming you center around only the regions where you feel like your Spouse misses the mark, you'll keep on seeing regions in which your Spouse misses the mark.

In any case, assuming you search for things to be grateful for about him, you'll see those things begin to develop and they'll become more straightforward and simpler to see.

Try not to contend that your accomplice is off-base when they request what they need. On the off chance that they're saying it, that is the manner by which it feels to them. On the off chance that you disagree, your responsibility is to sort out why it feels as such to them (in any case, obviously, without asking cross examining "why" questions).

I intruded on Bill's counter and showed him what I believed that him should do all things being equal. I asked Courtney a few explaining inquiries:

"Courtney, when's the last time you felt like you were investing quality energy with Bill?" When she gave me a model, I then, at that point, inquired, "What explicitly about that time caused you to feel associated?"

This is where the meat is people! Since, it wasn't actually necessary to focus on how much time you spend, yet the nature of that time. It seems like "quality time" while it's Connecting Time! Truly, when you invest seriously Connecting Energy with your accomplice, you'll find that they really set less expectations of your time, not more.

7. Talk about and Deal with Problems, Don't Let Go

We previously let you know this is an extremely normal misstep spouses do. In the event that you are pained by something, examine it. In the event that you are discontent with his way of behaving, examine it. In the event that you believe he should follow through with something, discuss it. You understand. Try not to cover your concerns under the ax. We are not requesting that you squabble. Moment outrage will just compound the situation. Quiet down before you introduce the issue and talk helpfully, without making allegations.

You really want to know how to discuss a relationship issue. The significant thing is to figure out how to permit the feelings in question.

Since keeping away from profound torment in your relationship neutralizes you.

Bad sentiments between you don't disappear all alone. You want to see them and calm them as a team, so they resolve. That is one significant capability of a sound relationship.

At the point when we stand up of outrage, we're set out toward inconvenience. Nothing bad can be said about saying something is irritating you. However, the way to being a decent accomplice is to discuss what you really want not your accomplice's flaws. And furthermore, figure out how to speak with your better half without raising your voice.

Additionally, you're not in a dreamland, and your romantic tale won't ever be pretty much as wonderful as what you read in fantasies and it's

OK. A piece of fixing your relationship's concerns is perceiving that what you have is somewhat flawed and it doesn't need to be. Acknowledge the way that you and your better half are simply people fit for settling on some unacceptable choices. Try not to cut off the friendship since you accomplished something wrong or your Spouse messed up. Kindly discussion about the main problems, recognize that you in all actuality do commit errors, and gain from them.

At the point when you two face a misconception over a specific issue, similar to when you can't settle on a joint choice, the best response is to talk things through. Correspondence is the brilliant key to making a relationship last, particularly while attempting to tackle an issue that influences both of you. Discuss it first and attempt to comprehend what turned out badly. It's ideal to talk about the issues together as opposed to battling and looking for someone else to take the blame.

Tell your accomplice your contemplations, and permit them to voice out their thoughts also. There's compelling reason need to demonstrate who has the better assessment on the grounds that, by the day's end, neither of you would be content with a weak choice.

Talking things through helps a ton, notwithstanding, as you dive deeper into your thought process as people and how you can concoct a split the difference over that subject you have been quarreling about.

8. Get some information about His Day Empathize

Recollect how you both used to talk about and take apart your days when you meet at night? Feels like ages back, correct? These days, the second he returns home, you are recently feeling better that there are an additional two sets of eyes and legs and hands to assist you with the child! This is almost certainly evident. However, put in no time flat to ask about his day. He may be feeling the squeeze from work - conversing with you could help him and give him an external viewpoint. He could have had a little progress in his work - he should impart the joy to you. Praise his triumphs and stand by him through his troublesome times. Like you promised to during your wedding.

9. Revive Your Sex Life

For some mamas, sex is the keep going thing on the psyche for quite a while. While you ought to take things slow, and do it just when you are actually and sincerely prepared for it, you want to talk about something very similar with your mate. As opposed to saying no consistently to him, discuss your interests and talk about how to handle them.

Furthermore, more significantly during the beginning stage of marriage, many couples scarcely surface for oxygen because of the energy of becoming hopelessly enamored. Tragically, this ecstatic state doesn't endure forever. Researchers have found that oxytocin (a holding chemical) delivered during the underlying phase of fixation makes couples feel euphoric and turned on by actual touch. It really works like a medication, giving us quick rewards that tight spot us to our sweetheart.

Clasping hands, embraces, and delicate touch are incredible ways of confirming your adoration for your accomplice. Actual fondness makes way for sexual touch that is centered around joy. Relationship specialist and instructor Dr. Kimberly Martin suggests that you put forth an objective of multiplying the time frame you kiss, embrace, and utilize sexy touch if you need to work on your marriage.

Physical allure is difficult to keep up with after some time. For example, Kendra and Jason need enthusiasm since they are reluctant to surrender control and show weakness. Therefore, they stay away from sex and seldom contact one another.

"Most sexual worries come from a relational battle in the marriage."

"Exploring new territory makes a feeling of holding and closeness. Consider fresh and do a movement that could startle you or energize you, similar to an entertainment mecca ride or a departure room. You will make dopamine and copy similar sentiments you had in the special night period of your relationship.

Specialists say dopamine and different synthetic substances in the mind are straightforwardly connected to actual fascination and heartfelt energy, which is the reason holding over another movement together could assist with starting excitement.

10. Cooperate together as one

Marriage is forever. Like a very much directed symphony, both you and your Spouse need to play your parts well as one to find true success. For doing this, you really want to obviously comprehend the new jobs and obligations that you have as parent. Plunk down, talk about and characterize these jobs. When you know plainly the parts you want to play and have high expectations about the parts your companion plays, your days will become clearer with less vulnerabilities. It will likewise make you all a group!

So, women, recall. Parenthood certainly is a God's approval - and you want to commit yourself completely to it - however not at the expense of your marriage. So go on, show a few loves and sneak in some sentiment.

We at Being the Parent wish you a cheerful wedded life, mom!

At the point when you initially met your life partner, you had a common fascination with each other in view of specific likenesses. Maybe you met while associated with an action which appeared to show that you had a few shared interests and objectives. You dated, fell head over heels, and wedded. Be that as it may, after marriage something changed. You started to see that you additionally had numerous distinctions which made clashes and division between you. As of now, you started to understand that you expected to make specific acclimations to recover the friendship and solidarity that you recently appreciated. Quite possibly of the best craving any two or three has is to encounter love, congruity, and genuine friendship with each other.

In any case, the inquiry is, how might you recapture friendship and fill together as one in your relationship? What are a few down to earth advances you can take to arrive at this objective? There is one rule that sticks out and is rehashed ordinarily in Scripture: the standard of arrangement. To find the concordance you want you should look for concurrence with your mate as the means to the objective of congruity and genuine friendship in your marriage. With each issue that emerges and each choice that is made, God believes you should look for concurrence with your mate. This rule was educated by Paul when he talked about dynamic in the closest part of marriage, the sexual association. He said, "Don't deny each other besides with assent for a period, that you might give yourselves to fasting and petition; and meet up again so Satan doesn't entice you in view of your absence of discretion" (1 Cor. 7:5). The word assent in this entry means to concur amicably.

On the off chance that you want congruity and unity with your companion, finding understanding is the means to this objective. Without arrangement there can be no enduring amicability between you. Accordingly, in every one of the areas of contention you are encountering at present, inquire as to whether this is your longing. Could it be said that you are trying to find arrangement together or would you say you are just looking for your own particular manner? .

At the point when you have contrasts that partition you there is just a single method for tracking down understanding and reestablish the concordance you want, and that is by finding a split the difference with each other. Compromise is accomplished when the two accomplices make concessions that empower them to track down center ground. On the off chance that there has been a new clash with your life partner in which your mentalities, words, or activities were hostile, you really want to start the compromise cycle by first going to your companion and admitting your shortcomings regarding this situation, and afterward request pardoning.